TIME FOR KIDS

STRANGE BUT TRUE

Bizarre Animals

Timothy J. Bradley

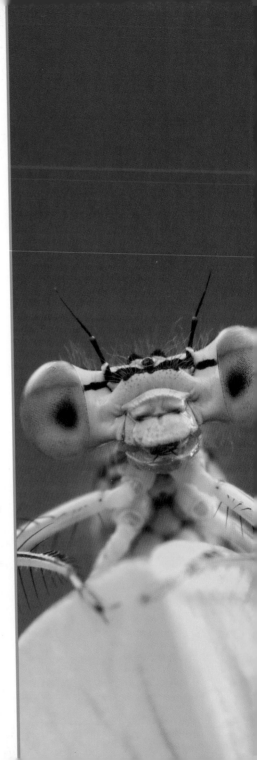

Consultants

Timothy Rasinski, Ph.D.
Kent State University

Lori Oczkus
Literacy Consultant

Tejdeep Kochhar
High School Biology Teacher

Based on writing from
TIME For Kids. *TIME For Kids* and the *TIME For Kids* logo are registered trademarks of TIME Inc. Used under license.

Publishing Credits

Dona Herweck Rice, *Editor-in-Chief*
Lee Aucoin, *Creative Director*
Jamey Acosta, *Senior Editor*
Lexa Hoang, *Designer*
Stephanie Reid, *Photo Editor*
Rane Anderson, *Contributing Author*
Rachelle Cracchiolo, *M.S.Ed., Publisher*

Image Credits: pp.14–15, 18–19, 22 (left), 24–25, 37 (top) Alamy; p.18 (left) AP/Corbis; p.22 (right) Dreamstime; p.9 (bottom) Getty Images/Photo Researchers, Inc.; p.39 (top) Getty Images/Science Faction Jewels; p.9 (both middle) Getty Images/ Visuals Unlimited; pp.7 (top), 16 (bottom), 26 (bottom), 28–29 iStockphoto; pp.30–31, 34 (top), 45 National Geographic Stock; p.36 Caters News Agency/Newscom; p.12 (left) Newscom; pp.9 (top), 10 (left), 13–14 (both left), 34–36 (all bottom) Photo Researchers, Inc.; pp.38–39 Timothy J. Bradley; All other images from Shuttertock.

Teacher Created Materials

5301 Oceanus Drive
Huntington Beach, CA 92649-1030
http://www.tcmpub.com
ISBN 978-1-4333-4861-7
© 2013 Teacher Created Materials, Inc.

Table of Contents

Why Are Animals So WEIRD?

Nature can be strange. Very strange. Many animals seem **bizarre** to us. Giraffes have long necks. Elephants have huge ears and long trunks. Rhinoceroses have sharp horns. And these animals aren't even the strangest!

What makes some animals so weird? It's all because of **evolution**. Creatures need to adapt in order to survive. Some animals live in harsh places such as the desert or deep in the ocean. Over time, they must evolve. They develop **adaptations** that help them survive in this wild world. These adaptations may seem weird to us, but these animals couldn't live without them.

THINK LINK

1 What adaptations help animals survive?

2 How do extreme environments cause animals to evolve?

3 In what ways are humans bizarre animals?

Baffling Bugs

Arthropods have developed some creepy features to help them survive. These critters have lived on Earth for over 500 million years. Scientists believe they were the first creatures to live on land. And now they can be found almost every place on Earth.

Insects are a type of arthropod. They are **invertebrates**. They have an **exoskeleton**, a segmented body, and jointed legs. Everything from a common brown spider to a crab is an arthropod. This group of animals includes some of the strangest species on Earth.

arthropod fossil

Grasshoppers use their legs to hear!

Incredible Insects

Today, the Goliath beetle is one of the largest insects on Earth. It's about the size of a computer mouse. And millions of years ago, dragonflies nearly two feet long flew through the sky!

Actual size!

Peppered Moth

Our world is always changing. And every creature must adapt to survive. Evolution occurs when animals change over time and increase their chances of survival. The peppered moth once spent its days resting on light-color trees. Its black-and-white wings blended in perfectly. But then the **Industrial Revolution** changed the world. People began using more machines. These machines produced pollution that filled the air. The light-colored trees became covered in dark soot. The peppered moth needed to adapt to the new environment. Some moths evolved darker wings and bodies. The darker moths were better able to hide from predators. In time, only black moths remained. This change didn't happen overnight. It took more than 50 years. But it allowed the peppered moth to survive.

Changing Colors

The peppered moth changed from white to black through 50 years of evolution. The moths that were best suited to the new environment survived.

Flower Mantis

The praying mantis is one of the fiercest predators on Earth. It waits to strike until its prey is near. Then it moves with amazing speed. With its spiny arms, it can capture prey that is much larger than itself.

Some mantises have evolved amazing forms of **camouflage** (KAM-uh-flahzh). The flower mantis looks just the way it sounds—like a flower! There are many species of the flower mantis. Some have legs that look like flower petals. They attract bees looking for pollen. But these bees are in for a cruel surprise. Those petal-like legs snap shut like a steel trap!

pink orchid mantis

conehead mantis

I'm called a *praying mantis*. I got my name because my front legs are bent. Humans say it reminds them of a person kneeling on the ground to pray. But don't confuse *pray* with *prey*. *Prey* describes a yummy snack. That's my favorite kind.

Spikes on the legs help the mantis pin its prey.

spiny flower mantis

ghost mantis nymph

Camouflage

Animals can be very quiet and very still. But camouflage is the best way for animals to blend in with the environment. Sometimes, animals need to hide from predators. Other times, they want to avoid being seen by their prey. Whenever camouflage is used, it gives animals a head start in the race to survive.

The snowshoe hare is famous for its white fur. During the winter, it blends in with the snow. In the spring, it will become brown again.

Stingrays hide their gray bodies under layers of sand in the water.

12

Humans use camouflage during war. By wearing clothes that blend in with the land, it's easier to avoid enemies.

Some ocean creatures like this nautilus are **countershaded**. They are dark on the top but light underneath. The light underbelly looks like the sun shining through the water.

A lion's mane matches the dry, yellow plants of the African grasslands.

Pink Cyanide Millipede

   Some arthropods are camouflaged, but the pink **cyanide** (SAHY-uh-nahyd) millipede isn't one of them. This two-inch-long millipede is a shocking-pink color. The bright color isn't meant for hiding. Instead, it's a warning to predators. The color says to stay away. This creature has an effective defense against predators. When threatened, it oozes **toxic** cyanide. Those who have studied the creature say it smells like almonds—a common sign of toxicity in the wild.

Poison!

Cyanide is highly toxic to humans. Victims must be treated immediately to avoid death.

Back Off!

Aposematism (uh-POZ-uh-ma-tism), or the use of warning colors, is found in many creatures. A bright color warns predators of a bad taste or poison. The predator remembers the bitter experience and avoids the nasty taste and bright color in the future. Warning colors are displayed by many different kinds of creatures, including poisonous frogs.

The pink cyanide millipede is a recent discovery. Scientists first discovered it in 2007.

Giraffe-Necked Weevil

The island of Madagascar lies off the coast of Africa. An odd little beetle lives there. The giraffe-necked weevil is barely one inch long. But just like the more famous African giraffe, it has a very long neck. Its long, skinny neck and bright red wings make it easy to identify. Males fight over the females, using their extra long necks to wrestle with each other. These tiny animals spend their lives in forest trees.

The female's neck is almost three times shorter than the male's neck. She uses her neck to roll a leaf into a tube. One egg is laid inside the tube. Then, she puts the leaf nest in a safe spot in a tree or on the forest floor.

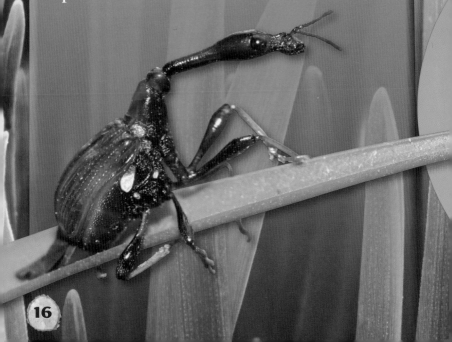

Giraffes also use their long necks to wrestle!

Baffling Beetles

Almost half of all known insects are beetles. Many beetles have weird adaptations.

Male rhinoceros beetles have huge horns on their heads. They use them to fight with other males.

Some scarab beetles are metallic. Light reflects off their bodies. This makes it easier for them to hide in between plants.

Tiger beetles are shockingly fast hunters that can run over five miles per hour. That's like a human sprinting over 510 miles per hour!

Mind-Blowing Mammals

Scales? Beaks? Webbed feet? Laying eggs? These are not traditional mammal traits. Most mammals don't lay eggs; they give birth to live young. Most have hair, not scales. And most mammals don't need webbed feet to help them swim.

But some mammals have developed weird adaptations to help them survive. Adaptations that help animals survive are passed on to their **offspring**. The adaptations that make it harder to survive are less likely to be passed on to offspring.

pangolin

Freaky Fact

Humans are mammals. But unlike most mammals, we have evolved to stand on two feet and are highly intelligent.

kangaroo

red panda

Tarsier

They may look like aliens. But these small mammals are well adapted to live in the jungles of Southeast Asia. They are **nocturnal** hunters. They feed on insects and other small animals. At night, the tarsiers call back and forth to each other to defend their territory.

They have huge, sensitive eyes. Each eye is as big as its brain. Those big eyes help the tarsier hunt in the dark of night. The eyes are so big that they can't move them. The tarsier must turn its head to look at something. Their ears move constantly, searching for sounds of danger. Tarsiers also have very long fingers and toes, which help them climb trees and pounce on their prey. Long tails help them keep their balance.

An owl has two huge eyes close together on the front of its face. The position of the eyes helps the owl judge the distance to its prey.

Like other insects, a dragonfly has compound eyes. Each eye has nearly 30,000 lenses.

Earthworms have eye spots that can only sense light and dark. This helps them find the dark, cool areas and stay out of the hot sun.

Pangolin

Pangolins are the only mammals with scales. They are made of **keratin**, the same material that makes up human fingernails and hair. When they are threatened, they curl into tight balls and let off a harsh smell. The edges of the scales are sharp enough to injure an attacker. Only the face and underbelly are not protected by scales.

These armored animals have a long tongue that is perfect for **lapping** up ants. Their front claws are so large that they curl them under when they walk so they won't be damaged. They bring them out when it's time to rip into an ant nest. The long tail is used for balance when crawling through trees. These timid creatures tend to live alone.

The name *pangolin* comes from a Malayan word meaning "rolling over."

It's a Grind

Pangolins don't have teeth, but they do have a gizzard-like stomach that grinds up their food for digestion. They swallow small stones and sand to help their stomachs break down food. These **gastroliths** aren't digested. When they become smooth from use, animals vomit them out and swallow new, sharper rocks.

Platypus

The platypus is a mammal that looks like a cross between a duck, a beaver, and an otter. It has traits that are similar to birds, reptiles, and mammals. Its strange mix of adaptations is perfect for its environment. One of the most unusual features of the platypus is that it lays eggs like a bird or a reptile. But it is a mammal because it feeds its young milk from its body.

The platypus lives in eastern Australia and spends much of its time in the water looking for food. It feeds on worms and insects. The bill of a platypus is flexible and rubbery. Webbed feet help it travel underwater. The back claws of the male platypus are **venomous**.

Strange but True

When scientists first discovered the platypus, they thought it was too strange to be real. They thought someone had played a joke on them!

Island Intrigue

Because it is so **isolated**, Australia is home to some of the most bizarre animals in the world. Wombats, echidnas, emus, and koalas are just some of the strange animals found in Australia.

wombat

echidna

emu

koala

Perfect Parts

The platypus is perfectly adapted to its environment. Take a closer look at its peculiar parts.

A platypus's tail is thick and flat. It stores extra fat and helps the animal swim.

The male platypus has venomous claws on its hind feet that can cause a painful injury.

The feet are webbed, which makes it easy to paddle through the water.

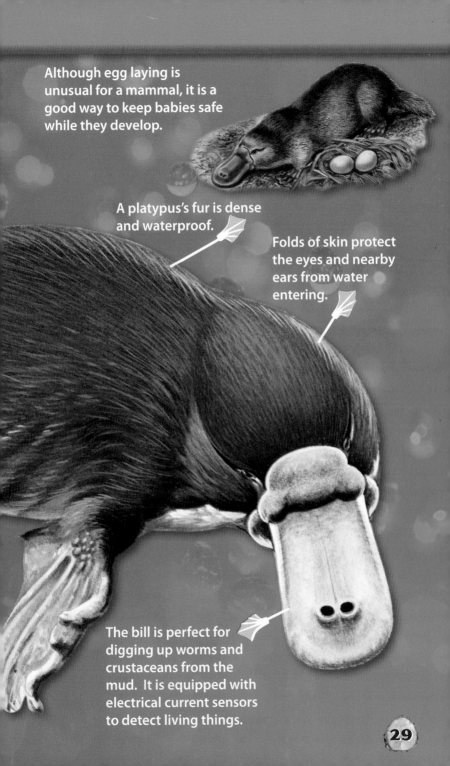

Although egg laying is unusual for a mammal, it is a good way to keep babies safe while they develop.

A platypus's fur is dense and waterproof.

Folds of skin protect the eyes and nearby ears from water entering.

The bill is perfect for digging up worms and crustaceans from the mud. It is equipped with electrical current sensors to detect living things.

Aye-aye

Aye-ayes live on the island of Madagascar. These odd creatures can be found in the canopy of the rain forest. They prefer to live high in the trees and rarely touch the ground. Like many creatures, they are active at night and rest during the day.

Aye-ayes have a special adaptation that helps them hunt. The third finger on each hand is long and thin. They use it to tap tree branches while looking for food. The tapping sound changes when they find small insects living inside the branch. Then they chew into the branch with their long teeth. Using their thin finger, they reach inside to dig out the meal.

Some people find the aye-aye to be so bizarre it's frightening. They tell legends of the aye-aye being a demon. They say it can kill by pointing its long eerie finger.

Specialized Hunters

Aye-ayes and woodpeckers have something in common. They both hunt for insects that live inside trees and tree branches. Aye-ayes use their fingers. Woodpeckers use their pointy bills. They peck at the wood to get at the insects inside.

Big Brains

Brains use a lot of energy. That means animals with bigger brains must spend more time and energy finding food. But bigger brains also make it easier to find food. Over time, many animals have developed larger brains that allow them to perform complex tasks. Scientists believe that bigger brains help animals adapt to changes more quickly. And there seems to be a strong connection between brain size and intelligence.

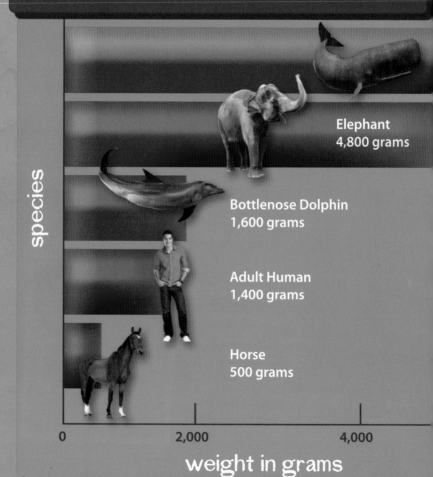

species

Elephant
4,800 grams

Bottlenose Dolphin
1,600 grams

Adult Human
1,400 grams

Horse
500 grams

0   2,000   4,000

weight in grams

Note: A gram is equal to .0022 pounds.

Sperm Whale
7,800 grams

STOP! THINK...

- In what ways do you think brain size is related to intelligence?

- Why do you think some animals are successful with smaller brains?

- How do you think we can recognize intelligence in other animals?

Humans may not have the biggest brains, but we have the most complex brains. Our brains have developed language, tools, and other skills that help us survive.

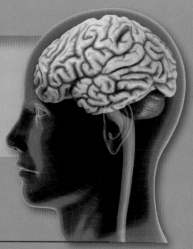

6,000   8,000

Freaky Fish

Life has existed in the ocean for millions of years. Thousands of species live in the cold, dark waters miles below the ocean's surface. Sunlight doesn't reach that far down. There is no plant life and little for them to eat. Instead, they rely on unique adaptations to help them survive in this underwater desert. They live on **sulfur** and **methane**. They eat the **remains** of other creatures. These are true survivors.

giant isopod

pelican eel

phantom anglerfish

Blobfish

The blobfish isn't the best looking fish in the ocean. But it's one that's hard to forget. This odd-looking fish lives in a dangerous **habitat**. Thousands of feet below the surface of the ocean, food is hard to find. It has no choice but to save its energy.

The blobfish is well adapted to this world. Its body is jelly-like and contains little muscle. Since its body is slightly less dense than water, the blobfish can float through the water. To catch its food, the blobfish just remains still and snaps up prey as it drifts by.

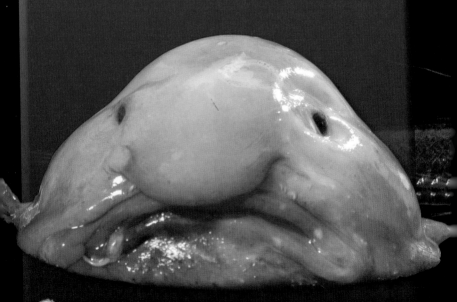

anglerfish

Ugly but Useful

The blobfish is just one of many deep-sea **organisms** that have developed bizarre bodies. Anglerfish carry glowing "lures" that attract prey right into their mouths. Viperfish have needle-like teeth so long they don't fit in their mouths. Even though these adaptations seem strange to us, they are what the creatures need to survive in the deep, dark blue.

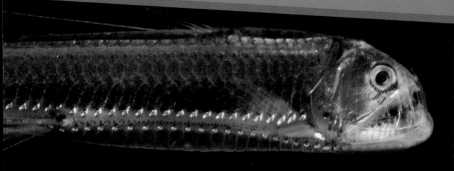

Sloane's viperfish

Barreleye

The barreleye is one of the most unusual deep-sea fish. Its huge eyes are perfect for seeing in the dark. Its tubular eyes are able to swivel up and look through a **transparent** dome. With these eyes, the barreleye can see prey floating above it. It may help to collect more light for better vision. What look like small, beady eyes on the front of the barreleye's face are actually scent organs that act like nostrils.

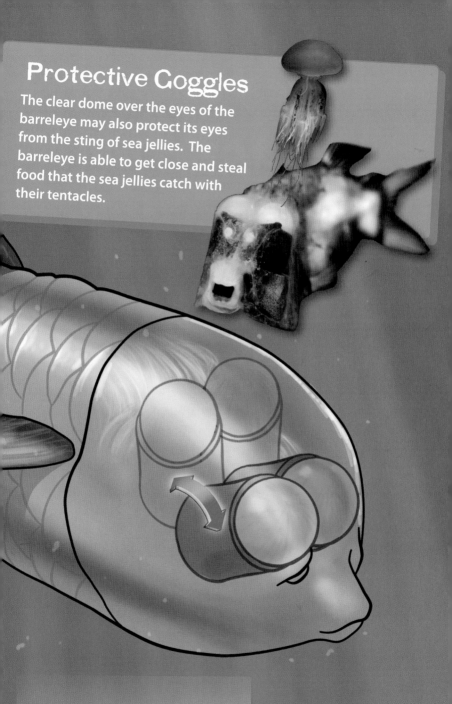

Protective Goggles

The clear dome over the eyes of the barreleye may also protect its eyes from the sting of sea jellies. The barreleye is able to get close and steal food that the sea jellies catch with their tentacles.

The barreleye fish is sometimes called a *spookfish*.

The Power of Adaptation

Animals don't decide to evolve. Adaptations happen randomly inside a creature's **DNA**. DNA is a set of instructions found in every cell. Those instructions tell organisms how they should grow and act. Some changes in DNA make animals weaker. Other changes make animals stronger. A slightly longer neck may make it easier to reach food. Larger eyes may mean it's easier to find prey. And larger ears can help an animal hear danger and escape more quickly. Over time, these small changes add up to a new species. They may look strange. But for these bizarre animals, these adaptations are the difference between life and death!

Red-eyed tree frogs are good climbers, with feet and toes adapted to their lifestyle.

A giraffe's long black tongue helps it reach the highest leaves.

Glossary

adaptations—changes in an organism that make it better able to survive in its environment

aposematism—the use of color to warn predators of poison

arthropods—animals with segmented bodies, jointed limbs, and a shell

bizarre—strange or weird

camouflage—coloration or shape that helps to hide something

countershaded—a color pattern where the top of something is darker than the underside

cyanide—a toxic substance

DNA—the material in every animal that tells the body how to grow and develop

evolution—the process that describes how organisms change over time

exoskeleton—a hard protective layer on the outside of an animal's body

gastroliths—pebbles or stones that are swallowed to aid in digestion over a long period of time

habitat—where organisms live

Industrial Revolution—a period in history that occurred in the 18th century when machines began to be used widely

invertebrates—creatures with no backbone or spine

isolated—alone or set off from others

keratin—the material fingernails and claws are made of

lapping—bringing in liquid with the tongue

membrane—a thin, soft flexible layer of plant or animal tissue

methane—a gas that is produced by the Earth and decaying matter

nocturnal—active during the night

offspring—the young of an animal or a person

organisms—living things

remains—what is left over or left behind

sulfur—a chemical with a strong smell that is poisonous to humans

toxic—poisonous

transparent—clear enough to be seen through

venomous—having or producing poison for protection or to catch prey

Index

Bibliography

BishopRoby, Joshua. *The World of Animals.*
Teacher Created Materials, 2008.
Find out how scientists classify animals, including those that are familiar and those that are strange.

Chinery, Michael. *Wild Animal Planet: Birth and Baby Animals.* **Anness, 2008.**
This book compares the life of insects, reptiles, birds, and mammals. Readers learn how various species develop skills to survive from birth through adulthood.

Collard, Sneed B. III. *Creepy Creatures.* **Charlesbridge Publishing, 1997.**
This book explores some of the reasons why animals are the way they are. These animals don't try to scare us on purpose. They are just trying to survive.

Davies, Nicola. *Extreme Animals: The Toughest Creatures on Earth.* **Candlewick, 2009.**
This funny, informative book describes some of the heartiest life forms on the planet, from the bacteria living inside volcanoes to the squash-proof creatures of the deepest seabeds.

Settel, Joanne. *Exploding Ants: Amazing Facts About How Animals Adapt.* **Atheneum Books for Young Readers, 1999.**
This book describes a variety of unusual creatures that survive by damaging or killing other animals.

More to Explore

American Museum of Natural History
http://www.amnh.org/ology

Discover more bizarre animals by clicking on *Biodiversity*. Download a field guide, play games, and explore unusual habitats at this online museum.

Mr. Nussbaum
http://www.mrnussbaum.com

Click on the *Science* section near the top. Use the Insect Generator and a Mammal Maker to piece together different parts of familiar animals to create your own bizarre bugs, complete with adaptations.

Amazing Animal Senses
http://faculty.washington.edu/chudler/amaze.html

Find out more about how animals use their senses to survive and experience the world in ways humans can only imagine.

Project Noah
http://www.projectnoah.org

This amazing project was launched in 2010 with the goal of documenting all the world's organisms. It even has a mobile application so you can take and submit photos with a smart phone.

Shedd: The World's Aquarium
http://sea.sheddaquarium.org/sea

This website has links to lessons, interactive activities, and facts about water animals, ecology, and conservation.

About the Author

Timothy J. Bradley grew up near Boston, Massachusetts, and spent every spare minute drawing spaceships, robots, and dinosaurs. That was so much fun that he started writing and illustrating books about natural history and science fiction. He loves to create new creatures based on real bizarre animals. He also worked as a toy designer for Hasbro, Inc., and designed life-size dinosaurs for museum exhibits. He lives in sunny Southern California with his wife and son.